Forty Whacks: Did Lizzie Borden Take an Axe?

EDGAR LUSTGARTEN

1

The charge against Lizzie Borden was inconceivable. That was the enduring strength of her defence. No matter how cogent the evidence, no matter how honest the witnesses, how could anyone credit the prosecution's case? That a woman, gently bred and delicately nurtured, should plan a murderous assault upon her stepmother; that she should execute it in the family home with such ferocious and demoniac force that the victim's head was smashed almost to pulp; that, having gazed upon her sickening handiwork, she should calmly wait an hour or more for her father to return; that she should then slaughter him with even greater violence so that hardened physicians shuddered at the sight; that neither loss of nerve nor pricking of remorse seemed to follow in the wake of such unnatural butchery—this was a tale that not merely challenged, but defied belief. It was like asking one

3

to accept the testimony of others that a horse recited Shakespeare or a dog had solved an anagram.

2

Everything combined to make this strain upon credence almost insupportable. At the eighteenth century's lowest moral ebb, some slatternly wanton such as [English painter William] Hogarth drew might have done these murders in a fetid slum, and still relied on incredulity giving the most unthinking jury pause. But this was not the eighteenth century; it was 1892. It was no strumpet of the streets who faced her trial, but the well-respected daughter of a well-respected man. And the setting of the scene was not Gin Lane or Seven Dials, but Fall River, Massachusetts, deep in the heart of puritan New England. Fall River at that time was a pleasant enough place, about the size of modern Cambridge, and not unlike a University town in its strong sense of community. People took close interest in other people's business. The leading citizens and chief officials were known by sight to all. Town matters wagged more tongues than national politics, and Fall River natives recognised as aristocracy, not the remote Four Hundred of New York, but the old Yankee families dwelling in their midst.

To this local elite belonged the Bordens, with Andrew Jackson Borden at their head. He was a prosperous businessman and banker who, through a union of acumen and avarice, steadily increased his considerable wealth. He chose to live, however, in rather modest style. His first wife having died when he was forty, he presently wedded one Miss Abby Gray and, with her and the two daughters of his former marriage, took up residence in a house on Second Street. It was a narrow house standing in a narrow garden, hemmed in by other houses on almost every side, with its front door only a few feet from the traffic and bustle of a much frequented thoroughfare. In a sense, nothing was lacking: downstairs had a sitting room, a dining room and a parlour; upstairs had a guest room and a dressing room for Mrs. Borden besides a separate bedroom for each of the two girls. But there was space without spaciousness, convenience without luxury, and both inside and out the house was unimposing if one remembered that this was the abode of a rich man.

In August 1892 the Bordens had been living there for about twenty years. Andrew was almost seventy. His wife was sixty-four. Miss Emma was forty-one. Miss Lizzie was thirty-two.

Before Miss Lizzie reached the age of thirty-three, this sedate and unexciting gentlewoman had made her name a lasting household word.

3

To all outward appearance the Borden house harboured a tranquil and contented household. But the façade was deceptive. Behind its look of blank correctitude lay deep antipathies and painful tensions.

The causes, though various, were intimately allied. There was the unattractive nature of the master; with his niggardly ways and autocratic temper, old Andrew inspired dread rather than affection. There was the classical aversion to the presence of a stepmother; the second Mrs. Borden, though amiable and harmless, could not engage the goodwill of Andrew's daughters. And as the latter grew up, their bitterness developed in the shape of jealousy and squabbling over property—jealousy that sprang from already strained relationships, squabbling that shadowed those relationships still more. The time came when Miss Lizzie, sharper-spoken of the sisters, pointedly dropped the appellation 'Mother' and adopted the formal 'Mrs. Borden' in its stead.

The division in the family intensified and hardened. As years went by, Miss Emma and Miss Lizzie evolved a technique to avoid their parents' company. Downstairs in the common rooms some contact was inevitable, but they contrived to reduce this to a satisfactory minimum by altering the times at which they took their meals. Upstairs it was much simpler. By bolting a single communicating door, the first floor could be split up into independent parts, one served by the front stairs, the other by the back.

On both sides of this door the bolts were permanently drawn.

4

The Massachusetts summer is uncomfortably hot. That of 1892 was no exception to the rule, and Fall River sweltered through those long July days during which dogs are reputed to go mad.

Late in the month Miss Emma left for Fairhaven, where she had arranged to spend a holiday with friends. At the same time Miss Lizzie paid a visit to New Bedford, but was back again at home before the week was out. In the sultry, stifling nights that followed her return, four people slept at the house on Second Street: Miss Lizzie, the old couple, and the servant, Bridget Sullivan, who occupied a room on the attic floor above.

On Wednesday, August 3rd, the four increased to five. Uncle Morse, a brother of the late Mrs. Borden, arrived unexpectedly to stay a night or two. He found Andrew and his wife a little out of sorts; whether through the heat, or through some less obvious cause, in the previous night both had been seized with vomiting, and, though better, were still not free from physical malaise. Lizzie, too, they told him, had been similarly affected, but in that divided and disservered house Uncle Morse was not to see his niece till nearly noon next day.

By then any thought of this mild indisposition had vanished in the stress of far more terrible events.

5

August 4th, 1892, is a memorable date in the history of crime. At the Borden home, where the grisly drama was to be enacted, the morning opened normally enough. The older people were all early risers, and seven o'clock found them sitting down to breakfast, prepared and served by the young Irish maid. The sun climbed swiftly into a clear sky; the air was heavy with the heat of many weeks; all signs portended, rightly as it proved, that they were in for another scorching day. All the more reason to perform one's chores before the torrid blaze of afternoon.

By nine o'clock Uncle Morse had left the house to

visit relatives elsewhere in the town. By nine fifteen Mr. Borden had set out on his round of business calls. Mrs. Borden had got a feather duster and was occupying herself with her household duties.

Meanwhile Miss Lizzie had made her first appearance. At nine o'clock she came into the kitchen where the servant Bridget was washing up the dishes. Bridget asked her what she fancied for her breakfast, but Miss Lizzie didn't seem to fancy very much. Having helped herself to a cup of coffee, she sat down to drink it at the kitchen table.

When the dishes were finished, Bridget took them to the dining room. There Mrs. Borden was assiduously dusting. She had noticed that the windows had got dirty and asked Bridget to wash them as her next domestic task.

Bridget decided to wash the outsides first. She got a brush and some cloths, filled a pail with water, and went out through the side door, which she left unlocked.

Mrs. Borden stayed inside. So did Miss Lizzie. The sun beat down with pitiless persistence and a drowsy silence fell upon the house.

6

At the partition fence Bridget stopped for a gossip with the maid next door. Then she started on the window-cleaning, working her way methodically around the house. She naturally looked into each ground-floor room in turn. She saw nobody in any.

The outside washing took perhaps an hour. Bridget then went back into the house, carefully locking the side door behind her. The Bordens were fussy about things like that, being morbidly fearful of robbers and intruders.

Everything was quiet; no one was about. Upstairs, taking it easy, Bridget enviously thought; best thing to do, on a broiler such as this. Conscientiously, she started on the inside of the windows....

At a quarter to eleven there was a noise at the front door; fumbling with a key and rattling of the lock. Must be Mr. Borden. Bridget dropped her cloths and ran to let him in.

She found the front door not only locked but bolted. As she struggled to get it open so as not to keep the master waiting, somebody behind her laughed out loud.

Bridget glanced over her shoulder. Miss Lizzie was standing at the top of the staircase, a few feet from the open door of the guest room. What moved her to mirth at that particular moment must ever be a theme for speculation; whether it was the spectacle of a flustered Bridget, or whether it was some hilarious secret of her own. . . .

When Mr. Borden was finally admitted, Miss Lizzie came downstairs.

'Mrs. Borden has gone out,' she volunteered. 'She had a note from someone who is sick.'

Her father made no comment. It was hotter than ever, and he had still not shaken off the after-effects of that mysterious illness. His walk around town had tired him more than usual. He went into the sitting room to rest.

Bridget was now doing the windows in the dining room. Miss Lizzie joined her there. She brought in an ironing board, put it on the table, produced some handkerchiefs and commenced to iron.

For a space the two women worked away in silence. Then Miss Lizzie asked a casual-sounding question.

'Are you going out?'

'I don't know,' Bridget said, energetically polishing, 'I might and I might not.'

'If you go out,' said Miss Lizzie, 'be sure and lock the door, for Mrs. Borden has gone out on a sick call and I might go out too.'

'Miss Lizzie, who is sick?' the maid enquired.

'I don't know. She had a note this morning; it must be in town.'

The windows were finished. Bridget withdrew into the kitchen, where she washed out the cloths. Presently, Miss Lizzie followed her.

'There's a cheap sale of dress goods on downtown,' she remarked. 'They are selling some kind of cloth at eight cents a yard.'

'Well,' Bridget said, 'I guess I'll have some.'

But at the moment Bridget did not feel inclined for out-of-doors. She had been up since six and kept hard at it ever since. A lie on the bed would make a nice mid-morning break....

In her attic box, Bridget yawned, stretched herself and relaxed. On the sitting room couch old Andrew, spent by his exertions, fell asleep. Once again the house lay in the stillness of that drowsy quiet.

7

The alarm was given fifteen minutes later. Bridget,

daydreaming beneath the baking roof, heard her name called somewhere far below. Even at that distance, though, she caught the note of urgency. She jumped up at once and called out to know what was the matter.

'Come down quick,' Miss Lizzie's voice floated up through the house. 'Come down quick; Father's dead; somebody came in and killed him.'

Dumbfounded and mistrusting her own ears, Bridget ran down the back stairs as fast as she could go.

Miss Lizzie was standing close to the side door. Bridget made as if to go into the sitting room, but Miss Lizzie checked her—perhaps to spare her feelings.

'Don't go in. I've got to have a doctor quick.'

Doctor Bowen lived opposite. Bridget flew across the road, leaving Miss Lizzie sole guardian of the dead.

The doctor arrived and went straight into the sitting room. He was to describe what he saw there later on the witness stand. 'Mr. Borden was lying on the lounge. His face was very badly cut, apparently with a sharp instrument; it was covered with blood. I felt of his pulse and satisfied myself that he was dead. I glanced about the room and saw there was nothing disturbed; neither the furniture nor anything at all. Mr. Borden was lying on his right side, apparently at ease, as if asleep. His face was hardly to be recognised by one who knew him.'

8

The news spread like wildfire. As police and officials hurried to the house, a crowd of gapers packed the street outside, eager for any sight or sound connected with calamity.

Dr. Bowen had to force a passage through this throng when he came out of the gate. He had covered Andrew Borden's body with a sheet; there was no other service he could usefully perform; now, at Miss Lizzie's personal request, he was going to the post-office to telegraph Miss Emma. Mrs. Borden, he had gathered, had gone upon some errand, and all they could do was wait for her return. Poor woman, Dr. Bowen thought, as he watched the gathering thicken; wherever she is, she'll hear the tidings soon enough.

He dispatched the telegram and gloomily made his way back towards the house. As he entered, a neighbour of the Bordens caught his arm. Her face was grey and her hands shook uncontrollably.

'They have found Mrs. Borden,' she said huskily.

'Where?' asked the doctor.

'Upstairs,' said the neighbour. 'In the front room.'

It was Miss Lizzie's suggestion that had prompted them to search; 'I'm almost positive,' she said, 'I heard her coming in.' It was Bridget and the neighbour who discovered Mrs. Borden, lying lifeless and mangled on the guest room floor. Her body was growing cold, and the blood which enveloped her mutilated head had already become matted and practically dry.

The doctors concluded that when Andrew Borden died his wife had already been dead more than an hour.

9

If the case had stopped short there, if no charge

against anyone had ever been preferred, Massachusetts would still have gone through weeks of ferment. If some hobo, some outcast, had been taxed with the crimes, his trial and the verdict determining his fate would have furnished all America with months of keen discussion. But when (after seven days of correlating evidence, during which the incredible gradually took shape) Fall River police arrested Lizzie Borden, the case at once acquired an entirely different stamp. It transcended the limits of geography and fashion; its range in time was perpetuity, in space the globe.

10

The trial of Lizzie Borden, delayed by various formalities of the law, took place at New Bedford in June 1893. It lasted thirteen days.

English readers, recalling the farce at Monkeyville or the spirited court scenes filmed in Hollywood, might pardonably expect the Borden trial to yield its quota of slapstick and burlesque. On the contrary. From first to last, at all times and all levels, the proceedings were conducted with a native dignity seldom attained in any land or age.

Three judges sat upon the bench: Chief Justice Mason, Mr. Justice Blodgett and Mr. Justice Dewey. For the Commonwealth (equivalent of the Crown) was Hosea Knowlton, the District Attorney, aided and partnered by William Moody, a colleague imported from an adjacent area. George D. Robinson, a former Congressman and ex-Governor of the State, with Andrew Jennings and Melvin Adams made up the team engaged for the defence.

To the modern eye, which finds a whiskered barrister hardly less freakish than a bald musician, there would have been something richly comic in the fine display of fringe, moustache and beard visible on counsels' row at Lizzie Borden's trial. But the advocates who sported these adornments were far from comic figures. They were masters of their complicated craft: shrewd in tactics, dexterous in argument, keen in cross-questioning, eloquent in speech. The defence, while energetically contesting every point and seizing every benefit admitted by the rules, took care in doing so never to depart from the highest standard of forensic practice. The prosecution, while making no effort to conceal the reluctance and distaste with which they entered on the case, did not suffer this to influence or impede the effective discharge of their melancholy duty.

In contrast to the custom observed in English trials, junior counsel played a prominent part. They were not confined to calling a few unimportant witnesses; they shared the speeches, and sometimes the cross-examination. As Knowlton was reserving himself for later responsibilities, it fell to William Moody to open for the Commonwealth.

11

Moody's speech was diffidently phrased, as befitted a naturally modest second string. He had frequent recourse to the protective 'I believe' and to the half-apologetic 'We fix that as well as we can.' But there was no cause for diffidence in the evidence he outlined. Before he had finished it was clear to demonstration that the Commonwealth had moved only on very solid ground. Their case was widely as well as firmly based on proof of motive, indications of design, circumstances pointing to exclusive opportunity, and acts by Miss Lizzie which (it could be argued) were only reconcilable with consciousness of guilt.

The motive broached, of course, was hatred of the stepmother, and concern for the destination of the father's substance. Counsel crystallised the bitterness that had inspired the former by referring to a slight but illuminating incident. It had occurred in the house on the morning of the murders while the bodies were still lying there in piteous quiescence. The Assistant City Marshal had arrived upon the scene, and in fulfillment of his office was questioning Miss Lizzie. 'When did you last see your mother?' he had asked. 'She is not my mother, sir,' Miss Lizzie had replied. 'She is my stepmother. My mother died when I was a child.'

To support their second proposition, that the prisoner was plotting and contemplating murder, the Commonwealth relied upon a curious conversation which had taken place between Miss Lizzie and a friend. On the eve of the catastrophe, while old Andrew and his wife spent their last night on earth entertaining Uncle Morse, Miss Lizzie went across town to see Miss Alice Russell, with whom for some time she had been on familiar terms. Miss Russell soon observed that her companion was depressed, and apparently a prey to morbid fears and fancies. 'I cannot help feeling,' she said, 'something's going to happen.' Miss Russell tried to dissipate this mood by cheerful logic, but Miss Lizzie stubbornly declined to be persuaded. 'Last night we were all sick,' she said. 'We are afraid we have been poisoned.... Father has so much trouble with men that come to see him, I am afraid that some of them will do something to him. I expect nothing but that the building will be burnt down over our heads. The barn has been broken into twice.' 'That', said Miss Russell soothingly, 'was boys after pigeons.' 'All right,' said Miss Lizzie, 'but the house has been broken into in broad daylight, when Bridget and Emma and I were the only ones at home. I saw a man the other night lurking about the buildings, and as I came he jumped and ran away. Father had trouble with a man the other day; there were angry words, and he turned him out of the house.'

Miss Lizzie's foreboding that 'something' was going to happen might have been premonition or sheer coincidence. But the Commonwealth, taking the conversation as a whole, invited the jury to accept a different view that she was cunningly diverting suspicion onto others in respect of crimes she herself meant to commit.

The prisoner's opportunity of accomplishing both murders was plain and incontestable on the admitted facts. But the Commonwealth were able to take this a step further. It was not only that *Miss Lizzie* had had ample opportunity; was there any opportunity for *anybody else?* The other members of the household were ruled out; Emma was in Fairhaven, Uncle Morse was with a niece more than a mile away, Bridget at the time of the second murder was upstairs. If it was not Miss Lizzie, then it must have been an intruder. There had been no entry by force. And, assuming for the moment that someone could get in and out completely unobserved, where were the signs that anyone had done so? Nothing was disturbed. No property was taken. No drawers had been ransacked. Mr. Borden's watch and money—more than eighty dollars—were left upon his person. What then was the motive prompting someone from outside? Was he perhaps one of those men Miss Lizzie spoke of to Miss Russell who had come to pay old Borden out after some angry clash? Then how came it that there was not the slightest evidence of a struggle? Old Andrew may have been asleep upon the sitting-room couch, but his wife would hardly go to sleep upon the guest-room floor. And yet, said Moody, 'the assailant, whoever he or she may have been, was able to approach each victim, in broad daylight, and without a struggle or a murmur, to lay them low.'

12

Motive fixed; design set forth; opportunity established. But there still remains the weightiest part of the prosecution case: the *behaviour* of Miss Lizzie that day and the days after. Upon three matters especially the Commonwealth pressed hard: one, the note from the unidentified sick person; two, the variations in Miss Lizzie's story; three, the burning of the light blue figured dress.

The business of the note is perhaps the most damning single point against the prisoner. 'Mrs. Borden has gone out,' says Miss Lizzie to her father, at the moment when he may go looking for her around the house. 'She had a note from someone who is sick.' There can be no denying that was what Miss Lizzie said; she admitted it herself when examined at the inquest. She had not, she deposed, seen the note with her own eyes, but Mrs. Borden told her of it, without naming the sender. Hence her own statement when her father returned home—a natural passing-on of domestic information. But the Commonwealth would have none of it. 'That statement,' declared Moody, 'we put forward as a lie; it was intended for no purpose except to stifle enquiry into the whereabouts of Mrs. Borden.'

It is the grave and awful fact that neither note nor sick person ever came to light. The implications for the prisoner are appalling, and, try as they would, the defence could not avoid them. The Commonwealth, not surprisingly, came to elevate the note to the most vital place of all, and it formed the subject matter of a powerful passage in the long speech which constituted Knowlton's winding up. 'My learned associate said in opening that that statement was a lie. I reaffirm that serious charge. No note came; no note was written; nobody brought a note; nobody was sick. Mrs. Borden had not had a note. *I will stake the case,*' said the District Attorney, *'on your belief in the truth of that proposition....* Little did it occur to Lizzie Borden when she told that lie to her father that there would be eighty thousand witnesses of its falsity. My distinguished friend has had the hardihood to suggest that somebody may have written that note and not come forward to say so. Why, Mr. Foreman, do you believe there exists in Fall River anybody so lost to all sense of humanity who would not have rushed forward without anything being said? But they have advertised for the writer of the note which was never written and which never came....

The whole falsehood of that note came from the woman in whose keeping Mrs. Borden was left by Andrew Borden, and it was false as the answer Cain gave to his Maker when He said to him, "Where is thy brother Abel?" '

Cain had answered, 'Am I my brother's keeper?' Lizzie Borden had not waited to be asked. 'Mrs. Borden has gone out. She had a note from someone who is sick.'

Maybe she was more free from sin than Cain. Maybe she was just smarter.

13

That morning of August 4th, as person after person—the maid, the neighbours, the doctor and the police—learned from Miss Lizzie's lips that she had found her father killed, each in turn was moved to ask her: 'Where were you?' It was not a query rooted in suspicion, but an instinctive reaction to something unexplained. Had she been out, had she repaired like Bridget to a remote part of the house, that she saw and heard nothing of the assault or the assailant?

Where were you? Miss Lizzie faced this question more than half a dozen times. Moody closely analysed her answers. To Bridget she had said: 'I was out in the backyard. I heard a groan, came in and found the door open and found my father.' To Mrs. Churchill, first of the neighbours to arrive, she said: 'I was out in the barn. I was going for a piece of iron when I heard a distress noise, came in and found the door open and found my father dead.' To Dr. Bowen she said: 'I was in the barn looking for some iron.' To Miss Russell she said: 'I went to the barn to get a piece of tin or iron.' To one officer she said: 'I was out in the barn for twenty minutes.' To another she said: 'I was upstairs in the barn for about half an hour.' To a third she said: 'I was in the barn and heard a noise like scraping.'

Now, hunting for what are called 'discrepancies' is a favourite occupation of legal pettifoggers [practitioners who are inferior or who employ dubious practices]. Such gentry often may be heard to say that they have 'been through the statements with a fine tooth-comb', and they proudly point out the results of their tooth-combing some trivial variation of emphasis or phrase. But statements made at different times by a really honest person hardly ever exactly correspond. Conformity is the offspring of deliberated art.

This consideration would not be ignored by able, up-right men like Moody and his leader. Their criticism was thus not primarily directed at the variations catalogued above. They took a more effective point—that later, when the flurry of that day had passed and Miss Lizzie produced a full, detailed account, she departed in a genuinely essen-tial particular from what she had said in her earlier re-plies. Three times at least in those first hours of confusion she had told of hearing some kind of a noise; a groan, a 'distress noise,' a noise like something scraping—but at any rate a sound that had attracted her attention, drew her back into the house, and so led to the discovery. But 'as enquiry,' Moody said, 'began to multiply upon her, another story came into view.... It is not, gentlemen, and I pray your attention to it, a difference of words here. In one case the statement is that she was alarmed by the

20

noise of the homicide; in the other case the statement is that she came coolly, deliberately, about her business (from the barn), looking after her ironing, putting down her hat and *accidentally* discovered the homicide as she went upstairs.'

However ingrained one's detestation of 'discrepancies,' one must concede the valid premise underlying this. In the upheaval following on the murders, the barn and the backyard may have seemed interchangeable and twenty minutes much the same as half an hour. But could you mistake how you had first made the discovery—whether a noise had sent you in already apprehensive or whether the hideous spectacle burst on you unawares? Could you forget whether the first alarm attracted eye or ear?

Unless Miss Lizzie was a liar and much worse, the answer is: you could.

14

The murders were committed on a Thursday. It was not till the next Sunday that Miss Lizzie burnt the dress.

There was no attempt at concealment or deception; no surreptitious happenings beneath the cloak of night. She acted quite openly, in daylight, before witnesses. For an innocent woman, her behaviour was extraordinarily naive; for a guilty one, it was extraordinarily stupid—or, as in the tales of G. K. Chesterton and Poe, extraordinarily clever in its very ostentation. For Miss Lizzie had been warned to pick her steps with care. On the Saturday evening the mayor of Fall River had expressly informed her that she was now under suspicion.

It was the following day, a little before noon. Alice Russell, who at this time was staying in the house, came down from the upper floor and went into the kitchen. There she found both Miss Lizzie and Miss Emma. The latter was busy washing dishes at the sink. Miss Lizzie was standing at the far end by the stove. She had a dress over her arm.

As Miss Russell came in, Miss Emma turned her head and said to her sister: 'What are you going to do?' 'I'm going to burn this old thing up,' replied Miss Lizzie. 'It's all covered with paint.'

She proceeded forthwith to tear it into strips.

There were several policemen on duty in the yard who could easily see in any time they chose to look. Miss Russell was so conscious of the equivocal effect created by this scene that she urged her friend at least to stand back from the window. 'I wouldn't do that,' she said, 'where people can see you.' Perhaps this remark took Miss Lizzie by surprise. At any rate, she did step a little out of vision— and placidly went on with the destruction of the dress.

The police, as Moody pointed out, had already searched the house and examined every garment to see if it was stained. They had found none marked with paint.

If the Commonwealth could have proved beyond a doubt that the dress Miss Lizzie burnt upon the stove was the dress she had worn on the morning of the murders, they would have pried loose the chief plank in her defence. *Not one who saw her on that convulsive morning had observed any blood upon her person or her clothes*, though—out of convention rather than necessity—neighbours had unhooked her dress, fanned her face and rubbed her hands. It was even more remarkable than in the case of Wallace. Wallace—on the assumption, for this purpose, of his guilt—had the house to himself while he washed and changed his clothes. He had to be quick, but he was safe from interruption. If Miss Lizzie committed these two sanguinary crimes ('the assailant would be spattered', said the prosecution expert), she would also presumably be bound to wash and change. But she must have done it *twice* and each time at the risk of being come upon by Bridget before all the traces of blood had been removed. And even if she ran that risk and, by the yardstick of success, justified her daring, how did she dispose of the incriminating clothes? After the second death, when the time margin was so narrow, they could only have been hidden somewhere in the house.

There lay the significance of the light blue figured dress which the prosecution sought to prove was the robe of homicide. But this was precisely what they could not do. Their witnesses disagreed among themselves about the dress Miss Lizzie wore upon the crucial day. Mrs. Churchill said one thing, Doctor Bowen said another, and neither Bridget nor Miss Russell could recall the dress at all.

Nonetheless, and notwithstanding its contradictory features, the Sunday morning episode in the kitchen was not one calculated to allay suspicion.

15

If, upon purely circumstantial evidence, you invite a jury to convict someone of murder, you must be ready

23

with the answers to all their unspoken questions. Moody had dealt with 'What for?' There still remained 'What with?'

Murders like these are not done with the bare hands, nor with any light and pocketable weapon. From some of the wounds on Andrew Borden's head, the length of the inflicting blade could be accurately fixed. It was three and a half inches, and it had fallen with the weight of a hatchet or an axe.

Where was this fearsome and death-dealing instrument?

It had not been abandoned at the scene of the crime. The murderer, therefore, had taken it away. Was it likely, Moody asked, that an intruder would have done so—that he would have run out with his bloodstained weapon into the sunlit street? Or did probability point to an inmate of the house, acquainted with its resources for concealment and disposal?

In the cellar, in a box upon the chimney shelf, the police had discovered a hatchet's head. The handle had been broken off, and the fragment that remained was covered with a coarse white dust of ashes. The blade of this hatchet had been measured. It was exactly three and a half inches long....

Here once again was deep suspicion that fell short of proof. The Commonwealth were appropriately reserved. 'We do not insist,' said Moody, 'that these homicides were committed with this hatchet. It *may* have been the weapon.' He paused. 'It may *well* have been the weapon.'

16

With force, and yet with moderation, the case against Miss Lizzie had been placed before the court. Moody's was a sound professional performance, and his distinguished leader looked on with approval as he began a final recapitulation.

'Gentlemen, let me stop and see where we are. The Commonwealth will prove that there was an unkindly feeling between the prisoner and her stepmother; that on Wednesday, August 3rd, she was dwelling upon murder, predicting disaster and cataloguing defences; that from the time when Mrs. Borden left the dining room to the time when the prisoner came downstairs an hour later from this hallway which led only to her chamber and that in which Mrs. Borden was found, there was no other human being present except the prisoner at the bar; that these acts were the acts of a person who, to have selected time and place as it was selected in this case, must have had a familiar knowledge of the interior of the premises and of the whereabouts and habits of those in occupation. We shall prove that the prisoner made contradictory statements. We shall prove that Mrs. Borden's was the prior death. Then we shall ask you to say whether any reasonable hypothesis except that of the prisoner's guilt can account for the sad occurrences on the morning of August 4th.'

The opening was over and so was the morning session. The court did not sit that afternoon. Members of the jury were otherwise engaged, exercising a privilege coveted by millions. In State-provided transport and accompanied by officials, they went off to Fall River to inspect the Borden home.

17

Next day the witnesses got into their stride, and defender Robinson got into his.

The ex-Governor was a jury advocate of natural talent and mature experience. He knew the world; he gauged people astutely; he had a flair for methods of approach. His mind was subtle, his expressions simple; he not merely understood others, he could make others understand.

In the Borden trial, his most important cross-examination was that of Bridget Sullivan, the Irish maid. It could hardly have been bettered.

Bridget was not by any means a vulnerable witness. She was neither fool nor knave. But, like most human beings, she was susceptible to suggestion and subject to mistake. Discreetly Robinson made his own suggestions; relentlessly he exploited her mistakes.

He began by seeking Bridget's help in challenging the idea that the Borden family was rent asunder by ill-feeling. How far he could go with this could hardly be foreseen, and it is worth observing how every question tests or prepares a foothold for the next.

'Did *you* have any trouble there?' he asked.

'I?' said Bridget. 'No, sir.'

'A pleasant *place* to live?'

'Yes, sir.'

'A pleasant *family* to be in?'

'I don't know how the family was,' said Bridget, 'I got along all right.'

This was a slight setback. It might even be a warning. Robinson explored with a sure but gentle touch, like a surgeon who comes upon some dubious obstruction.

'You never saw anything *out of the way?*'

'No, sir.'

Good; if she never saw anything 'out of the way' one might be a little bolder and more definite.

'You never saw any *conflict* in the family?'

'No, sir.'

Excellent; one could go the whole hog now, and put it into terms the jury couldn't fail to grasp.

'Never saw any *quarrelling*, or anything of that kind?'

'No, sir,' answered Bridget. 'I did not.'

Side note for those interested in the technique of cross-examination: Robinson's aim is clear. He achieves it with the last question of this sequence, when he gets Bridget to agree that she never say any 'quarrelling, or anything of that kind.' But he dare not ask this baldly, without careful preparation, because he cannot foresee the terms of her reply. Supposing she says, in response to a blunt query, 'Miss Lizzie and Mrs. Borden quarrelled all day long.' His cause will then be far worse off than if the matter had not been raised at all. So he needs to approach the question circumspectly, advancing only one step at a time, and at every stage leaving channels of escape which he can use without grave loss of face.

He starts with just one hard fact to work from. Bridget has been in the Bordens' service for close upon three years. That dictates the form of his first question.

'Did *you* have any trouble there?'

If Bridget says 'Yes,' Robinson can retort, without fear of contradiction, 'But you *did* stay there three years,' and then, accepting the danger signal, ride off to some less inflammable topic with a specious air of having scored a point. If Bridget says 'No,' as she does, he has strengthened his hand, improved his position, and gained a better sight of the ground ahead.

It does not take him very far. But it enables him to venture next on a question that appears superficially a mere rephrasing of his last. In fact, though, by an almost imperceptible change in stress, it is designed to bring him closer to his target.

'A pleasant *place* to live?' he asks.

This imports the idea that not only were things all right for Bridget personally, but the Borden household was all right in general. And yet he can be fairly certain that Bridget will say 'Yes' to this after her affirmative reply to the previous question. The two sound so alike. If, surprisingly, she does say 'No', Robinson's escape is open as before, but with additional virtue—'But you stayed there three years and you never had any trouble.'

This, however, does not arise. Robinson safely collects another 'Yes.'

Now he comes to the most delicate point in the sequence. He must ask, however broadly, about the family themselves. He has, it is true, buttressed himself by the two preliminary questions, but this is the danger spot, and he knows it.

'It was a pleasant *family* to be in?'

28

Bridget's answer raises a problem. A downright 'Yes' would have brought the advocate almost home. A downright 'No' would have driven him from the trail; it would have been far too dangerous to press her further. Robinson would have made off under cover of a volley of safe questions. ('Pleasant enough to make the place pleasant, eh?' 'Pleasant enough to stay three years with, eh?' etc.)

But Bridget's reply is enigmatic. 'I don't know how the family was,' she says. 'I got along all right.'

Is this to be taken at its face value? Or is she hinting that there were family dissensions and that she kept out of them? Robinson has gone a long way now; he does not want to withdraw without his prize. But the utmost care is called for.

The next question, so artless in appearance, packs into its small compass a lifetime's experience and skill.

'You never saw anything out of the way?'

'Out of the way' is exactly right. Respectable girls— and Bridget is a very respectable girl—do not describe places as 'pleasant' where 'out of the way' things occur—as Robinson will, if necessary, remind her. But Bridget gives no cause.

'No, sir,' she says.

Now he is practically secure. If any quarrelling is mentioned, they are ordinary, everyday domestic quarrels, quarrels that could not be considered 'out of the way'. He can go straight forward.

'You never saw any conflict in the family?'

Even if, contrary to expectation, Bridget should say 'Yes,' Robinson is well protected. But Bridget says 'No' and he reaches his goal.

'Never saw any quarrelling or anything of that kind?'
'No, sir.'...

And few of the spectators are aware that they have heard a little gem of the cross-examiner's art. *(End side note.)*

So far so good. The girl had seen no open wrangles. But Robinson wishes to take it a stage further, and dispel any belief in a purely passive feud. He tackled Bridget about the allegation that Miss Emma and Miss Lizzie held aloof from family meals.

'Didn't they eat with the family?' he asked.

'Not all the time.'

Robinson took this reply and turned it upside down.

'But they did from time to time, did they not?'

The meaning was the same but the effect had been changed. It was like substituting 'half-full' for half-empty.'

'Yes, sir,' Bridget said, somewhat doubtfully, and added, 'Most of the time they didn't eat with their father and mother.'

Counsel met her insistence with the utmost ingenuity.

'Did they get up as early as the father and mother?'

'No, sir.'

'So they had their breakfast later?'

A logician would have jibbed at the word 'so'. But George D. Robinson had the measure of his audience. The Borden jurymen would not be conversant with the fallacy of *post hoc propter hoc*. Absences from breakfast were credibly accounted for.

'And how was it at dinner?'

'They were sometimes at dinner,' Bridget said. 'But a good many more times they were not.'

'Sometimes they were out?' Robinson suggested.

'I don't know where they were; I could not tell.'

Bridget was digging in her heels. A whole string of gains may be sacrificed by ill-timed importunity. Smoothly the advocate altered his direction.

'Did you ever hear Miss Lizzie talk with Mrs. Borden?'

'Yes, sir; she always spoke to Mrs. Borden when Mrs. Borden talked to her.'

'Always did?' repeated Robinson, making certain they had caught it in the recesses of the jury box.

'Yes, sir.'

'The conversation went on in the ordinary way, did it?'

'Yes, sir.'

'How was it this Thursday morning after they came downstairs?'

Bridget wrinkled her forehead.

'I don't remember.'

'Didn't they talk in the sitting room?'

'Yes.'

'Who spoke?'

'Miss Lizzie and Mrs. Borden.'

'Talking calmly, the same as anybody else?'

'Yes, sir.'

This enabled Robinson to make a bigger throw.

'There was not, as far as you know, any trouble that morning?'

'No, sir,' said Bridget. 'I did not see any.'

In this phase of the questioning relations were quite

amicable. It would not have suited Robinson if they had been otherwise. But now a more acrimonious passage was impending.

The conception of a murderous intruder constituted a vital part of Robinson's defence. To account for the fact that between crimes One and Two an intruder must have remained upon the premises more than an hour, experiments had been carried out with the object of establishing that he could have concealed himself in a closet in the hall. But primarily he would have had to obtain access to the house; and this in practice was limited to periods during which the side door had been left unlocked. The more they were, and the longer, the better for Miss Lizzie.

Bridget, in direct examination, had fixed one; she owned to leaving the side door 'off the hook' while she was cleaning the outside of the windows. She agreed, too, with Robinson that, while she was engaged upon the windows in the front and while she was chatting to the next door neighbours' maid, the side door would be hidden from her view and—Robinson's words—'the field pretty clear for a person to walk in.'

All that was very well, but it was not enough. Robinson knew that a useful piece was missing. Earlier on the morning of the murders, Bridget had gone out, not to the front but to the yard; it would widen the scope for the conjectural intruder if she had left the door unhooked when she returned on that occasion. Many months before, at the inquest at Fall River, she had said she couldn't tell whether she did or not. With Miss Lizzie on trial for her life, Bridget had somehow recollected. 'When I came back from the yard,' she had asserted, 'I hooked

32

up the side door.'

Robinson did not propose to let this matter pass. Every minute that the side door might have been un-hooked was precious. Before she left the stand the girl was going to retract.

He picked up a bulky set of papers. It was a transcript of the evidence at the inquest.

'Do you think,' he said, and there was the faintest undertone of menace in his drawl, 'do you think you have told us today just as you told us before?'

'I have told all I know,' said Bridget.

'I don't ask you that.' The tone suddenly sharpened. 'What I want to know is whether you have told it today just as you did before?'

'Well, I think I did,' said Bridget, a shade taken aback. Mr. Robinson had seemed such an easy, pleasant man. 'I think I did, as far as I remember.'

'What did you do as to the side door when you came in from the yard?'

'I hooked it.'

'Did you say so before at the other examination?'

'I think so.'

'Do you *know* so?'

Bridget wavered.

'I'm not sure,' she said.

'Let me read and see if you said this.' He read aloud very slowly and distinctly. ' "Question: When you came in from the yard did you hook the side door? Answer: I don't know whether I did or not." Did you say so?'

'Well, I *must* have hooked it because—'

'That isn't it.' Robinson cut in without ceremony.

33

'Was that the way you testified?'

'I testified the truth.'

'I don't imply that you didn't.' It was indeed Robin-son's whole point that she did; that the truth about the hooking of the door had been given at the inquest and not at the trial. 'I merely want to know if you recall testify-ing over there at Fall River that you couldn't tell whether you hooked the door or not?'

But it stuck in Bridget's gullet.

'It is *likely* I did hook it, for it was always kept hooked.'

Robinson's face was very stern.

'Do you positively recollect one way or the other? '

'Well,' said Bridget, scared but obstinate, 'I *generally* hook the side door.'

'That isn't what I asked.' The ex-Governor was per-emptory. 'Did you hook it or did you not?'

'I know I *must* have hooked the door for I always—'

'That isn't it. Did you hook it or did you not?'

Bridget gave up.

'I don't know,' she said. 'I don't know whether I did or not.'

The spectators took a deep breath. Ex-Governor Robinson's frown relaxed. He looked almost affable again as he passed on to the next question.

18

At the luncheon breaks and afternoon adjournments, jurymen poked each other in the ribs. That ole Guv'nor Robinson; he puts it across; there an't no flies on him.

But the jury were out of court when he put it across best and when the absence of flies was most conspicuous. For Robinson's triumphs at getting evidence in were surpassed by his triumphs at keeping evidence out.

There was, for example, Mr. Eli Bence.

Mr. Eli Bence had a simple tale to tell. He was a drug clerk at a Fall River pharmacy. On August 3rd, sometime in the forenoon, Miss Lizzie, whom he knew, had come into the shop. She had asked for ten cents' worth of prussic acid—required, so she said, for cleaning sealskin furs. 'Prussic acid, my good lady,' Mr. Bence had replied, 'is something we don't sell without a prescription from a doctor. It is a very dangerous thing to handle.' Miss Lizzie had departed without her prussic acid.

The very name of this substance conjures up unnatural death; one might as well use the word 'poison' and be done. A picture of Miss Lizzie trying, *without success,* to purchase prussic acid on the day before the murders might easily provoke a prejudicial train of thought. Had she turned from one method of killing to another—from the inaccessible poison to the handy household axe?

Her defenders could not afford to sit back unconcerned while the ground was prepared for this damaging idea. If there was any way of stifling it, stifled it must be. So Mr. Bence had barely settled on the stand, having got little further than announcing his full name, when George D. Robinson rose from his place with a general objection to the witness being heard.

This objection, argued of course in the absence of the jury, was based upon two points. First, that prussic acid had harmless as well as harmful uses; 'it is an article,' said

Robinson, 'which a person may legitimately buy.' Second, that the attempted purchase could have no conceivable bearing upon murders with an axe—'and that is all we are enquiring about here.'

Moody, for the Commonwealth, faced this submission squarely. (It might be thought that Moody, as Knowlton's junior colleague, was doing rather more than his fair share of the work. But it would seem that a rough division had been mutually agreed; Moody was to open the case and argue points of law, Knowlton was to cross-examine and make the final speech. And in the trial of Lizzie Borden, as will presently appear, the final speech on each side assumed paramount importance.)

The Commonwealth spokesman seized at once on Robinson's last point—that the prussic acid episode did not prove, or tend to prove, that the defendant committed two murders with an axe. Quite right, Moody said; the evidence is not being offered for that purpose. It is meant to show intent, to demonstrate premeditation, to cast a revealing beam of light upon the prisoner's state of mind.

For Robinson's other point, the Commonwealth were well armed. They had brought to court a furrier and an analytical chemist to say that prussic acid was not used for cleaning furs. 'I can conceive.' said Moody, 'of no more significant act, nothing which tends to show more the purpose of doing mischief than the attempt, on an excuse which upon this proof was false, to obtain one of the most deadly poisons known to human kind.'

The judges conferred. They agreed with the Commonwealth where a layman might have hesitated—that proof of attempts to procure an instrument of murder might be introduced as evidence of intent even though the murder charged was subsequently effected with an instrument of quite a different kind. But they were doubtful where a layman might have felt no doubt at all— whether prussic acid could not be put to uses neither noxious nor medical.

They decided to hear the furrier and the chemist. These experts duly testified, and, while the jury still kicked their heels outside, there followed a long and whispered consultation between judges and counsel, who moved forward to the bench. There was much wagging of expository fingers and skeptical shaking of celebrated heads. It was noted that those concerned for the Commonwealth looked grave, while those for the defence looked inwardly exultant.

When at last the advocates returned to their seats, the judges proceeded to give a joint decision. There was insufficient proof to satisfy the court that the acid could not be used for an innocent purpose.

The poison evidence would therefore be excluded.

19

If Robinson had fought hard to keep out Eli Bence, he fought harder to keep out ... Lizzie Borden.

Miss Lizzie had already given evidence on oath—at the inquest, to which she had been summoned by subpoena. There, under Knowlton's cross-examination, she had proved an obstinate but unconvincing witness. The contradictions in her story were rife and absolute; the explanations few and often incomplete. She had been down-stairs in the kitchen when her father returned home; no, she had been upstairs, sewing on a piece of tape; no, she remembered, she had been downstairs after all. She had gone out to the barn to find a sinker for a fish line; she had not been to the barn before for possibly three months; she didn't know what made her choose that spe-cial, fateful moment; she had stayed up in the barn for a space of twenty minutes; it was a very hot day and the barn was dreadfully close; no, of course she wouldn't stay there any longer than she need. How long would it take to find the sinker—three minutes, or four? No, it took her ten. And the remaining ten, Miss Borden? She was just looking idly through the window of the barn, eating three pears she had brought in from the yard....

These and a score of other jarring incongruities made Miss Lizzie's testimony a danger to herself. It had been the clinching factor that had led to her arrest, and now the Commonwealth were tendering it at trial to be read out to the jury as evidence of her guilt.

But again her leading advocate entered an objection. Miss Lizzie's inquest testimony, he claimed, was inadmis-sible.

The rule relating to and governing such matters rested on a long line of American authorities. All really depended on the status of Miss Lizzie when, in obedience to the fiat of the law, she appeared at the inquest and submitted herself to questions. Was she then a perfectly free agent, an ordinary citizen, called to help the coroner determine cause of death? If so, even though she may have been under suspicion, her testimony was 'voluntary' and admissible. Or was she already in effect an accused person, called less to help the coroner than to answer for herself? If so, any statements made by her would not be 'voluntary' and could not be employed against her at the trial.

The inquest concluded on August 11th. Miss Lizzie was arrested later the same day. Until that moment she was, by presumption, free, but Robinson argued that the contrary was the fact. For three days past the City Marshal of Fall River had had in his pocket a warrant for her arrest. During the whole of that period she was under observation by police detailed for the purpose and stationed around the house. She was not cautioned before she gave her evidence. Her request for counsel at the inquest was refused. 'In other words, the practice that was resorted to was to put her really in the custody of the City Marshal, beyond the possibility of any retirement or release or freedom whatever; keeping her with a hand upon the shoulder, covering her at every second, surrounding her at every instant, empowered to take her at any moment, and under these circumstances taking her to that inquest to testify. Denied counsel, not told that she ought not to testify to anything that might tend to incriminate herself, she stood alone, a defenceless woman, in that attitude. 'If that is freedom,' Robinson exclaimed, 'then God save the Commonwealth of Massachusetts.'

Moody's reply was vehement and scornful. How, he asked, could an undisclosed warrant, of which the woman had no suspicion whatsoever, bear upon the exercise of her will when she appeared as a witness at the inquest? Where was there a grain of evidence to show that her liberty was restrained for an instant until the end of her examination? What authority had been quoted, could be quoted, to justify exclusion of such testimony unless the person testifying was actually under arrest? Moody attacked Robinson with almost spiteful sarcasm. 'I say of what my friend is pleased to call his argument: it is magnificent but it is not law.'

Law or no law, Robinson gained the day. 'The common law,' said the Chief Justice, 'regards substance more than form. It is plain that the prisoner at the time of her testimony was, so far as relates to this question, as effectively in custody as if the formal precept had been served. We are all of opinion that this is decisive, and the evidence is excluded.'

This did not debar Miss Lizzie from telling her story to the jurymen afresh. In Massachusetts, unlike Britain at that period, prisoners were permitted to give evidence if they wished. But Miss Lizzie did not intend to avail herself of this privilege. One encounter with Mr. Knowlton was enough.

20

With the acknowledged leading lady unwilling to perform, Miss Emma Borden became the star of the defence.

Here was indeed a most serviceable deputy. She could give much of Lizzie's story without running Lizzie's risk. She could tell the jury almost all her sister could have told about the prelude, the background, and the sequel to the crimes; but because on August 4th she had been away at Fairhaven, she could not be cross-questioned about the day itself. The substitution of the elder sister for the younger was a neat and effective tactical device.

According to the best theatrical tradition, Miss Emma's entrance was deliberately delayed. When at long last the Commonwealth rested (on the tenth day, in defiance of the Scriptures) the defenders first released a little swarm of witnesses each of whom contributed some item of his own. One, who lived just behind the Borden home, had heard a curious 'pounding' on the night of August 3rd. Another, who had passed the house early on the 4th, had seen a young fellow hanging around; he was pale and 'acting strangely.' A third, walking by a little later in the morning, observed an unknown man leaning up against the gate. Such evidence was flimsy, not to say remote, but shrewd George Robinson perceived a latent value in composing this sketch of an alternative assassin.

The jury spent some hours among these fanciful conjectures. When the big moment arrived, though, and Miss Emma took the stand, they were instantly plunged back into the cold harsh world of fact.

Miss Emma, whatever nervousness she felt, rose to the requirements of her exacting role. Her timing was precise. She described how her father always wore a single ring; how it had been given to him years ago by Lizzie; how it was the only jewelry he ever wore; how it was on his finger at the moment of his death and how it was still upon his finger in the grave. She described how thoroughly the police had searched the house and how Miss Lizzie never made the least objection. She described how her sister burnt the dress on Sunday morning, and said that *she, Miss Emma, had prompted her to do it*. 'The dress got paint on it in May when the men painted the house.... On Saturday, the day of the search, I went to the clothes press to hang up my own dress. There was no vacant nail. I searched 'round to find a nail and noticed this dress. "You've not destroyed that old dress yet," I said to Lizzie. She said: "I think I will," and I said: "I would if I were you." '

Miss Lizzie would certainly have done it far less well. George Robinson himself could not have done it better. The telegraph systems tapped it out across the world; the sister has come out strongly on Lizzie Borden's side.

21

In a long trial for murder, as day follows day and witness follows witness, even the participants may temporarily forget the agony of decision that awaits them at the end. They may become so immersed in the interplay of advocates, the interpreting of laws, and the balancing of issues that these processes come to appear ends instead of means—means by which twelve can arrive at a conclusion which will spell for one either liberty or death.

The completion of the evidence reawakens apprehension. As the last of many witnesses passes from the stand, the minds of all in court are increasingly preoccupied by hopes or fears of the fast approaching verdict.

At this stage the verdict can sometimes be foreseen. Not so, however, in the case of Lizzie Borden. The clash was less one of *fact* than of *construction*, less a matter of which witness you accepted than which counsel. It was a battle of barristers for command over the jury, and the outcome of that battle had yet to be decided.

22

Other things being equal, recent impressions are bound to be the strongest. That is why advocates contend for the last word. In the Borden trial the last word lay with Knowlton, because of the evidence that had been called for the defence. Robinson had to precede his opponent, with all the disadvantages attached to that position.

In his introduction to the transcript of the trial—an essay that stands high in the literature of crime—Mr. Edmund Pearson compares Robinson with Knowlton, and does not conceal his preference for the latter. It is true that Knowlton was animated by the loftiest sentiments and the noblest ideals. It is true that he spoke majestic prose with a splendid rhythm and an almost biblical ring. It is true that Robinson, by contrast, was homespun and colloquial, with both feet firmly planted on the Massachusetts earth. Nonetheless, I am convinced, he was the better advocate and had the more astute mind. He possessed what, for want of a better word, one may call *courtcraft*; he attuned himself exactly to the mental pitch prevailing; he neither preached to nor lectured nor apostrophised the jury, but *talked* to them about the case as a neighbour might at home.

Along these lines and within these limits, his final speech was a real forensic feat.

It is evident that throughout he kept in mind not only the logic of facts and of events, but the way the jury could be relied upon to *feel*. He began by playing on their natural reluctance to believe that a woman could have carried out these crimes; 'it is physically and morally impossible.' He traded on the human love of jeering at the police: 'They make themselves ridiculous, insisting that a defendant shall know everything that was done on a particular time, shall account for every moment of that time, shall tell it three or four times alike, shall never waver or quiver, shall have tears or not have tears, shall make no mistakes.'

Beside these matters of emotional propensity, he swept into place the one solid piece of evidence that told heavily and positively in favour of his client. 'Blood speaks out, though it is voiceless. It speaks out against the criminal. Not a spot on her, from her hair to her feet, on dress or person anywhere. Think of it! Think of it for an instant.'

Having laid this foundation of artistically commingled hypothesis and fact, Robinson turned to the prosecution's case. He took the points against him one by one, and in plain, familiar words, with nicely managed raillery, made all—or nearly all—appear paltry or fallacious.

'Why do they say she did it?' he enquired. 'Well, in the first place, they say she was in the house.' Already it sounded far less good a point than when it had been termed 'exclusive opportunity.' Robinson added to the ground so quickly gained. 'She was in the house. Well, that may look to you like a very wrong place for her to be in. But ... it is her own home. I don't know where I would want my daughter to be than at home, attending to the ordinary vocations of life, as a dutiful member of the household.'

The jury pouted their lips sagely. No doubt about that; she had a right to be at home. No, sir; couldn't say she was to blame for being at home.

Next, the Commonwealth had talked about a motive. Why, Robinson demanded, did they set great store on this? 'If a person commits a murder and we know it, there is no reason to enquire for what reason he did it. If he did it, then it does not make any difference whether he had any motive or not.... In this case the motive is only introduced to explain the evidence, and to bind her to the crimes.' And what sort of motive had they ultimately proved? They had shown that, from five or six years ago, Lizzie did not call Mrs. Borden 'Mother'—Lizzie, who was indeed her stepdaughter, and was now a woman thirty-two years old. They had stressed her correction of the Assistant City Marshal: 'She is not my mother, sir; she is my stepmother.' Robinson's comment on this was superbly opportune. He recalled to the jury 'a well-looking little girl' who had given some minor evidence on behalf of the defence. 'Why, Martha Chagnon, that was here a day or two ago, stepped on the stand and began to talk about Mrs. Chagnon as her stepmother. Well, I advise the City Marshal to put a cordon around *her* house, so that there will not be another murder there. Right here, in your presence, she spoke of her stepmother, and Mrs. Chagnon herself came on the stand afterwards, and I believe the blood of neither of them has been spilled since.'

It was the kind of illustration that a country jury loves: concrete, local, about people they had seen. They pouted again and shook their heads a little; didn't seem much in the stepmother business either.

The Wednesday evening talk between Miss Lizzie and Miss Russell—styled by the Commonwealth 'evidence of design'— was dismissed by Robinson as hardly worthy of discussion. 'There are a good many people who believe in premonitions.... Events often succeed predictions through a mere coincidence.... You all recollect that Miss Lizzie's monthly illness was then continuing and we know from sad experience that many a woman at such a time is unbalanced, her mind unsettled and everything is out of sorts and out of joint.'

'We know from sad experience.' It was another clever touch. The family men looked back into their own domestic lives, and the whole jury glowed with superior male strength.

The lawyers and reporters listening to the speech, who were well acquainted with George Robinson's quick wits, had never doubted his ability to score whenever circumstances offered the tiniest of openings. But they waited with deep interest to see how he would handle a matter in which they discerned no opening at all: the matter of the note 'from someone who is sick.'

The defender did not dodge the point; he could not if he would. And if it made the weakest part of a very powerful speech, no possible blame can be attributed to him.

'A person may say,' he said: ' "Where is the note?" Well, we should be very glad to see it. Very glad.' Nobody could doubt that this sentiment was sincere. If the note had materialised, it might have proved decisive. 'Very likely Mrs. Borden burned it up. But then they say nobody has come forward to say they sent it. That is true. You will find men living perhaps in this county who do not know that this trial is going on, don't know anything about it, don't pay much attention to it; they are about their own business; don't consider it of consequence. Sometimes people don't *want* to get into a courtroom even if a life is in danger.'

Robinson's manner was as confident as ever, but the content of his argument now wore a little thin. The jury looked puzzled. His grip on them was loosening. Up to now they had gone all the way with Guv'nor Robinson, but they didn't feel happy with this talk about the note. Did it make sense? They tried to imagine what they would have done themselves—the test that he was always asking them to apply. Would *they* not have known that the trial was going on? Would *they* have hung back, if it meant somebody's life? But there wasn't really time to think the problem out; Robinson was moving on to another, better point.

The Commonwealth had charged his client with inconsistent statements. 'The others tell us she said she went out to the barn. It's the police that tell us how long she said she stayed there. It takes Assistant Marshal Fleet himself to get the thirty minutes. You see him. You see him.' He pointed to this officer sitting there in court, stiff as a ramrod, haughty as a dowager, obsessed with his own distinction and importance. 'You see him,' said Robinson, like an enthusiastic teacher taking his pupils around a zoo, 'you see the set of that moustache and the firmness of those lips.' The moustache bristled, the firm lips set still tighter. 'There he was in this young woman's room....

47

This man Fleet was troubled. He was on the scent for a job. He was ferreting out a crime. He had a theory. He was a detective. And so he says: "You said this morning you were up in the barn for half an hour. Will you say that now?" Miss Lizzie said: "I do not say half an hour. I said twenty minutes to half an hour." "Well," says Assistant Marshal Fleet, "we will call it twenty minutes." ' Robinson's voice grew higher in derision. 'Much obliged to him. He was ready to call it twenty minutes, was he? What a favour that was! Now Lizzie has some sense of her own, and she says: "I say from twenty minutes to half an hour, sir." He had not awed her into silence. She still breathed, though he was there.'

Assistant Marshal Fleet had no option but to listen, and the jury could savour his discomfiture in safety. They chuckled with delight at the slights he was enduring. That ole Guv'nor Robinson had them back again in thrall.

Robinson now ranged to and fro on ground that was congenial: the burning of the dress (where Miss Emma lent him strength), Miss Lizzie's supposed attempts to tempt Bridget to town ('If she had undertaken these deeds, think you not she would have sent Bridget out on an errand?'), the Commonwealth's uncertainty about the murderer's weapon. Nor did he forget to offer his own theory. 'The side door, gentlemen, was unfastened from about nine to eleven.... Bridget was outside talking to the next-door girl; she couldn't see the side door when she was there. Lizzie was about the house as usual. What was she doing? The same as any decent woman does. Attending to her work, ironing handkerchiefs, going up and down stairs. You say these things are not all proved'—

Knowlton had stirred restlessly—'but I am taking you into the house just as I would into your own. What are your wives doing now?'

The jury felt homesick. They were suddenly out of this oppressive, crowded court; they had ceased to be the center of the waiting world; they were back there on the farm, with a cool breeze blowing and the missus putting on a good New England meal.

'What are your wives doing now?' Robinson's voice wound its way into their thoughts. 'Doing the ordinary work around the house, getting the dinner. Well, where do they go? Down cellar for potatoes, into the kitchen, here and there. You can see the whole thing. It was just the same there.

'Now suppose the assassin came there and passed through. Where could he go? He could go up into that bedchamber and secrete himself to stay there—until he finds himself confronting Mrs. Borden. Now what is going to be done? He is there for murder; not to murder her, but to murder Mr. Borden. And he knows that he will be recognised, and he must strike her down. A man that had in his mind the purpose to kill Mr. Borden would not stop at the intervention of another person, and Lizzie and Bridget and Mrs. Borden, all or any of them, would be slaughtered if they came in that fellow's way.

'And when he had done his work, and Mr. Borden had come in, as he could hear him, he could come down. Bridget was upstairs, Lizzie outdoors. He could do his work quickly and securely, and pass out the same door as he came in.'

Robinson had very nearly finished, but, like most

master advocates, he had nursed and husbanded his most dramatic stroke.

Steadily he gazed upon the close-packed jury box. His tones were level and imperative.

'To find her guilty, you must believe she is a fiend. *Gentlemen, does she look it?*'

The speech had gone full circle. 'Is it possible?' 'Does she look it?'

They looked, and saw Miss Lizzie with her high, severe collar; her modestly groomed hair; her long, slender hands and her sharp, patrician features; her unmistakable air of being, above all else, a lady.

They looked at her, and her advocate had played his strongest card.

23

To Knowlton this was the most difficult and disagreeable case of his career. Having placed his own evidence squarely before the court, having closely cross-examined the opposition witnesses, he must have been tempted to exert himself no further. A short and colourless concluding speech, from which it would appear that he was loath to press the matter, presented itself as the least unpleasant course.

But Knowlton was a man of rectitude and principle; his personal inclinations did not influence his conduct. As a government official he owed a duty to the public. It was a primary part of that duty to ensure that criminals did not escape their just and proper punishment. He believed, with some reason, that he had a strong case, and that it would be a dereliction of his high responsibility to neglect any lawful means of capturing the jury.

As Robinson sat down, amid that buzz of tongues which bursts forth uncontrollably on the slackening of tension, Knowlton slowly rose, like a man oppressed with care, and resolutely started on his grim, ungrateful task.

He grappled at once with the greatest of his difficulties. 'My distinguished friend says: "Who could have done it?" The answer would have been: "Nobody could have done it." If you had read an account of these cold and heartless facts in any tale of fiction, you would have said: "That will do for a story, but such things never happen.... It was an impossible crime." But it was committed. Set any human being you can think of, put any degraded man or woman you ever heard of, at the bar, and say to them "You did this thing," and it would seem incredible. And yet it was done; it was done.'

He particularly deprecated Robinson's suggestion that the murders could not have been committed by a woman, and permitted himself a few general observations on the temperament and nature of the female sex. 'They are no better than we; they are no worse than we. If they lack in strength and coarseness and vigour, they make up for it in cunning, in despatch, in celerity, in ferocity. If their loves are stronger and more enduring than those of men, their hates are more undying, more unyielding, more persistent.' In disdainful phrase he struck at a main obstacle to cool-headed decision. 'We must face this case,' he said, 'as men, not as gallants.'

Through the twelfth afternoon and through the thirteenth morning, Knowlton continued his remarkable ad-

51

dress; gravely exhorting, patiently explaining, impeccable in literary style and moral tone. His thesis was twofold: that Miss Lizzie's story was in itself incredible; that anybody else could have done it was impossible. It was beyond credence, he declared, that on that sweltering day she went up to the barn, 'the hottest place in Fall River,' and there remained all the time that Bridget was upstairs. It was beyond credence that, upon discovering her father, she had not fled from the house to the safety of the street; 'she did not know that the assassin was not there; she did not know that he had escaped.' It was beyond credence that the murder of Mrs. Borden could take place without Miss Lizzie seeing or hearing anything unusual; 'if she was downstairs she was in the path of the assassin, if she was upstairs only a thin deal door [a wooden door made of a plank of pine or fir] separated her from the crime.' It was beyond credence that a dress that had been good enough to keep through May, through June, through July, and into August should, innocently and by sheer coincidence, be destroyed twelve hours after she had heard of the suspicions. It was beyond credence that a mysterious assassin should know he would find the side door open at the exact time he desired, should hide in closets where there was no blood found, should come out when there was no opportunity to come out without being seen by all the world, should know Bridget was going upstairs to rest when she didn't know herself, should know Lizzie was going to the barn when she couldn't have told it herself, should know that Mrs. Borden would be upstairs dusting when no one could have foreseen it. 'What is the defence to our array of facts? Nothing; nothing. It is proven, Mr.

Foreman; it is proven.'

No passage in his speech was more impressive in its thoughtfulness and stunning in its horror than that in which he sought to analyse Miss Lizzie's motives. The order of the crimes, he said, supplied their key. He reversed Robinson's theory that the woman met her death through coming upon and recognising a murderous intruder who had got into the house to lie in wait for Mr. Borden. 'No,' said Knowlton, 'it was Mrs. Borden whose life that wicked person sought, and all the motive we have to consider bears on her.' And whatever might be said about old Andrew, except for Miss Lizzie (and the absent Miss Emma), his harmless wife had not a single foe. 'There may be that in this case,' said Knowlton very solemnly, 'that saves us from the idea that Lizzie planned to kill her father. I hope she did not. I should be slow to believe she did. But it was not Lizzie Borden who came down those stairs, but a murderess, transformed from the daughter, transformed from the ties of affection, to the most consummate criminal we have read of in our history. She came down to meet that stern old man. That man who loved his daughter, but who loved his wife too, as the Bible commanded him. And, above all, the one man in this universe who would know who killed his wife. She had not thought of that. She had gone on. There is cunning in crime, but there is blindness in crime too. She had gone on with stealth and cunning, but she had forgotten the hereafter. They always do. And when the deed was done, she was coming downstairs to face Nemesis. There wouldn't be any question but that he would know the reason that woman lay in death. He knew who disliked her. He knew

53

who couldn't tolerate her presence under that roof.'

As a work of abstract art, this speech of Knowlton's has surpassing merit. The language is choice, the mood exalted, the reasoning taut and deep. It is excellent to read. But the study is one place, the courtroom is another, and the best advocacy seldom makes the best literature. The jury, simple folk that they were, may well have found George Robinson more comprehensible. They may have felt more at home with his less august style.

Before he ended, Knowlton made a brave attempt to lift the issue of the trial onto a spiritual plane. 'Rise, gentlemen,' he cried, 'to the altitude of your duty. Act as you would be reported to act when you stand before the Great White Throne at the last day.... Only he who hears the voice of his inner consciousness—it is the voice of God Himself—saying to him "Well done, good and faithful servant," can enter into the reward and lay hold of eternal life.'

This peroration has real grandeur. It puts to shame George Robinson's humble 'Gentlemen, does she look it?' But one wonders which stood uppermost in the minds of the jury as they sat in their little private room deciding Lizzie's fate.

24

By five o'clock that afternoon it was all over. Miss Lizzie had been acquitted in a tempest of applause. With her faithful sister Emma at her side, she was on her way home to celebrate her vindication. George D. Robinson, well pleased with himself, walked away from court amid the cheering of the crowds. Only in the office of the District Attorney, Knowlton and Moody sat apart from the rejoicings. They alone, perhaps, were at that moment capable of beholding the Borden trial through the eye of history. Miss Lizzie lived thereafter for four and thirty years, with every indication of an easy conscience. She had inherited a comfortable fortune which she placidly and soberly and decently enjoyed. She never married. She occupied herself—as she had formerly done—with a variety of charitable works, and in her will she left thirty thousand dollars to a society for the prevention of cruelty to animals.

Her death let loose in public a flood of speculation that had gone on in private ever since the trial. Students of crime and detection endlessly debate: was the Borden verdict right?

Others remember Lizzie for a different reason. A catchy little jingle, probably written before she was acquitted, has linked itself imperishably with folk and nursery lore.

Lizzie Borden took an ax
And gave her mother forty whacks,
When she saw what she had done
She gave her father forty-one.

Students may argue about her as they please. In the wide world that is her epitaph.

ABOUT THE AUTHOR

Edgar Lustgarten (1907–1978) was a British broadcaster, criminologist and crime writer. In the 1950 and '60s he hosted the crime series *Scotland Yard* and *The Scales of Justice*. Other titles include such crime novels as *Blondie Iscariot* and *Game for Three Losers*, and such true crime works as *A Century of Murderers* and *The Illustrated Story of Crime*.